Spectral Realms

No. 17 ‡ Summer 2022

Edited by S. T. Joshi

The spectral realms that thou canst see
With eyes veil'd from the world and me.

H. P. LOVECRAFT, "To a Dreamer"

SPECTRAL REALMS is published twice a year by Hippocampus Press,
P.O. Box 641, New York, NY 10156 (www.hippocampuspress.com).
Cover art and design by Daniel V. Sauer
Hippocampus Press logo by Anastasia Damianakos.

ISBN 978-1-61498-387-3   ISSN 2333-4215

Contents

To Richard L. Tierney
1936–2022
in memoriam

Poems

Slouching toward Yuggoth

Richard L. Tierney

Out on the solar system's farthest rim
The tiny man-made capsule makes its way
Through regions where the feeble solar ray
Gleams like a fading star, distant and dim.
For years that capsule, at a dwindling pace,
Has been approaching a dark planetoid
Within the black, transplanetary void—
Dark Yuggoth on the rim of solar space.

Men dubbed it Pluto when it first was seen
By earthly eyes—a quite appropriate name,
For ancient tomes warned of its grim demesne . . .
I fain would swerve our capsule, damp its flame!
For, if espied, what strange rough Things might rise
And cross black space to plague terrestrial skies?

To Richard L. Tierney: In Memoriam

Leigh Blackmore

Thou devotee of Amerind's dark morn,
Can it be true that thou art laid to rest
From all thy ways amongst the rippling corn
Of thine own land whose ways thou loved the best?
Where hast thou gone—perchance to darkly dwell
Amidst Carcosa's dim and awful lair?
Or, snatched away with dread Dark Lord Zathog,
Beneath the strange black stars that circle there,
Do now some dim dark vortices explore
Where evil dreams and savage menace rule?
Perhaps in Mason City, through your door
There came the Blob That Gobbled up Abdul?
Or did the distant darksome Winds of Zarr
Catch you away too soon, fling you awhirl
From fantasy to dreadful cities far?
Perhaps Hell laughs as scrolls of Thoth unfurl
To sound thy fate, to hymn you to bleak rest
In Gardens of Lucullus; or with Wendigo
As drums of Chaos beat unhallowed, test
Your stride through sleet and snow.
Jest of Old Ones—"take him at the crest
Of all his powers, unto some blazing star!"
Night-blossoms now, beneath the sunset, flower;

The tatters of the King
Enshroud you as you speed unto your bower;
Of Gnosis dark, you sing.
Red Sonja lives, and Simon wields his blade
Against the might of Rome;
John Taggart travels time, still unafraid;
In many a hoary tome
Your verse lives still, its bitterness unmatched
Except perhaps by Bierce;
Yet even so, your worldview stands detached—
Both gentle notes and fierce.
A toast for you from Howard's Bran Mak Morn;
A raised, full glass from Utressor and Smith;
Night blossoms' perfume o'er the hills is borne;
Tsathoggua in his Toad-House croaks his myth.
The Hermitage is silent now; e'en so,
"Eldritchard" lives in memory—this we *know*.

The Sleep of Reason Produces Monsters: An Extended Surveil

Carl E. Reed

"Imagination abandoned by reason produces impossible monsters;
united with her, she is the mother of the arts and source of their
wonders."—Caption to aquatint #43 of the *Los Caprichos* series

The sleep of reason produces monsters,
warned Goya, who etched a stark aquatint:
an exhausted man face down at his desk
surrounded by owls, bats, lynx—a dark hint
of feral forces that stalk the artist:
sickness of the spirit personified.
'Ware, ye sterile cold men of abstraction!
Nature denied is falseness deified.
Mad wild men of Dionysus—far worse:
Id-driven, unmoored, Thanatos-enthralled.
Reason throttled is horror: iron law
of the dream-dazed, drunks, psychotics, et al.
Great art is grounded, insightful, precise;
it hallows, enlightens—rolls back the night.

A Promise for Today

Maxwell I. Gold

When the trumpets of someday blasted across the dead fields of yesterday, the plastic cities whose false promises of tomorrow were forgotten beneath worm and ruin. Dim, anacreontic choirs moaned, their voices simmering beneath broken streets and limp towers where the deranged ideologies of a race long since dead were now entombed in brick and calcified thoughts. I remembered so many awful years ago, when those dissonant tones smashed together in my ears as fire and the stubbornness of flesh met the immovable metallic gods, who cared not for the machinations of our species. It was a beautiful concordance, growing louder, higher until at its crescendo there was only ash and night. There was nothing I could do to stop it. To stop the spastic innovations, bloody promises, and worthless pursuits of self-damnation.

Death might have been a welcomed friend, but that friendship was forfeit long ago, only fodder for the worms while I was cursed to endure a fate worse than any other.

Despite my twisted perceptions, the nature of time escapes me. The circular nature of events had lost its value as most things decay, changing form and function within a cold universe. Fruitless, my efforts will go unheeded for whoever reads this as they wonder on the non-linear logic of a man who was unable precisely to articulate the end of days. How am I different from so many before me, who heard those great trumpets?

I find myself trapped today, in moments of broken space and fractured realities where the bodies of tomorrow and yesterday are tossed under baneful assurances that the trumpets of someday *will* blow.

La Gata

Lori R. Lopez

"Talk to La Gata."
I was led through a dark alley,
wondering if I'd see daylight again.
Embarked on a quest. Not fitting
in the ordinary world. Dysphoric,
at odds, I didn't wish to be human.
I wanted a tail, pointed ears.
I couldn't stand my bare skin!

There were rumors of a Cult
that welcomed those like me who
craved Metamorphosis. The M-Word.
Flesh tingling, I followed a catty
unchatty female into the shaft to
an underground realm defined by garish
graffiti, silhouettes, cat glyphs on walls.
A No Man's Land (or Woman's).

La Gata was a goddess, everything
I desired to become! The deformed
feline-feminine aspect, her smugly
intense gaze, the amber orbs and
fur-flecked complexion.
She led Cat Colony, recruiting
a wild pack to exist beyond the
parameters of Society and Norms.

"You are young." Even her accent
felt exotic, enticing. "Such change
bears a price. At an early age
the mind is not set. You would be
surprised how much you can still
transform without magick or other
means. Impressions, decisions,
experiences. You must wait."

A brusque dismissal, a gesture.
"Come back when you are truly
grown!" I struggled at the door.
"No! This is all I can think about!"
"Of course. Who doesn't want to
be something else at times?
We go through phases . . .
This isn't a game, a fantasy."

The Cat-Woman leaped toward me,
snarling, teeth grimacing, eyes
aglow. "It is a breaking of bones —
a destroying of your very nature!"
I shrank from the heat of her breath.
"You cannot switch back temporarily.

You cannot return to your old life.
You will cease to be."

Her bodyguard's grip on my arm
tightened. La Gata confronted me,
nose pressed to mine. "Understand.
The longer you are a cat, the more
uncivilized, instinctive, inhuman
you will behave. Ruthless. Savage.
Chimeric. That should not be
risked, unless absolutely certain."

I couldn't focus—eye to eye.
Was I certain? I couldn't think.
"You've heard of Werewolves
haven't you? Lycans transformed
from men. In these parts, if your
sister is bitten, she won't turn
into a dog. This is her fate!
But it is permanent. Forever."

A claw pricked my cheek.
"Full-Moon or broad daylight.
Meow!" Her fanglike teeth
exposed, threatening. A fierce

smile expanded lips. "There is
a golden aura for Gatas and silver
aura for Lobos. The two factions
battle. Arch-enemies."

Her claw stroked the base of my
chin. "Still here? I can always use
warriors. You will be trained in
the Feral Arts. Cat-Fighting."
She attacked, sinking those cusps
into my shoulder. I howled,
then contorted. An excruciating
moment. Shockingly abrupt.

Like her shift in mood, her
change of mind. Like her . . .
I had converted to a beast,
impulsive, cunning, mercurial.
Both beautiful and horrible.
She was right. I am no longer
me. I have shed my life
to serve La Gata.

Footsteps in the Night

Ngo Binh Anh Khoa

Again I hear the tapping sounds of feet
Upon the floor, which softly tear into
The silence of the midnight hour and through
My sleep. Again my heart would wildly beat
Within my heaving chest, for in my home
At present there is no one else but me;
Whose feet are those that tread so tauntingly
Each night outside my room when I'm alone?
Some rats or burglars? No. The cameras spot
No sign of such, and now the footsteps ring
Much nearer, louder, much more maddening!
Then silence! In the grip of fear I'm caught,
Which numbs my body and consumes my soul,
When near my head two glaring red eyes glow.

The Golden Age

Charles Lovecraft

Our kings ride to the prow near bosomed maids,
The shapely bowsprits for whose laurels yearn;
Some use fierce dragonheads to fright the braids
Of enemies that Norsemen always spurn.

Through spume and ice-drift northern vessels earn
The wealth and honour that the cool clan trades;
While with sword prowess which the pagan learn
Grow tastes for blood and valour's accolades.

They are not lost for reckoning who sharp
And raven wits shall drive the clans across
To other shores, to plunder and to harp
On battles won that never reach to dross,
For hardy eyes and frosty beards usurp
All weakness, while the fallen foe finds loss.

I Met a Girl in a Cemetery

John Shirley

I met a girl in a cemetery
(I was there for a walk)
And oh, she's a gossamer beauty—
though silent when she talks

she smiled as we strolled along
she sang to me in her mind
somehow, someway I heard her say
that our stars were aligned

> *We knew each other,*
> *Though we'd never met,*
> *At least not in this life*
> *We knew each other*
> *For once we'd met*
> *On an ancient moonless night*

I caught her tender thoughts
Of our love in another life
And sadly she was thinking
that I never made her my wife

she sank into her lonely grave
singing, "Meet me far below—
in the cavern of the dead
where the hidden river flows . . ."

I See Too Much: A Clairvoyant's Complaint

Frank Coffman

My gift . . . my *curse* is that I see too much—
Not with my eyes, but with my "inner sight."
It haunts my days and wakes me in the night.
My vivid visions . . . always too late! Such
Is a source of agony, for they tend—
Though starkly clear, to show a scene of gore—
To show a tragedy, some poor soul's end.
Too late is worse than never, so before
My bane beholds another wretched death
That can't be thwarted—I will end this woe . . .
And pray that, when this body draws no breath,
That *Inner Eye* will close—where'er I go.
    Though I've helped Justice prove the evil deed,
    From this "gift's" torment I shall now be freed.

House

Rebecca Fraser

Where roof meets frame on windburned peak
Ancient bones extend and creak
Now woken from tormented dreams
The house pulls the threads of dying screams
And weaves them into every stud
To fill her veins with rotten blood
And all who tread her tainted halls
Hear wretched whispers from her walls
From corners dark where light can't breach
Skeletal arms from shadows reach
To clutch in anguish those who pass
Release us from the house's grasp
But those who enter never leave
Absorbed into each board and eave
They're drawn into the house's soul
And coalesce to make her whole.

Malice Must Dwell within Your Heart

Darrell Schweitzer

Whatever you conjure out of the midnight air,
whatever you summon from a corrupted grave,
for the sake of portentous prophecies,
is just shadow and a fading echo
unless malice dwells within your heart.

No witchcraft, no incantation, no tongue-twisting
recitation in a dead language,
no thousand pages of forbidden lore
can be anything more than pedantry,
unless malice dwells within your heart.

Let the flame of hatred burn pure and true.
Let it consume you beyond pleasure and pain.
Then shall your mummeries be as daggers.
Then can you call down death and doom,
As long as malice dwells within your heart.

The Nachzehrer

Scott J. Couturier

Buried one fortnight in unhallowed earth
following death by poison's burning wrack:
no priest to speak sanctification, dearth
of mournful farewells, of flowers a lack,
swarming flies solely reckoning her worth.

Now eye & jaw gape open wide, her shroud
devoured by famished & slurping degrees,
grave-clothes masticated with munching loud—
hungry for essence of her family,
a bloodline ancient, impious, & proud.

One by one they are stricken to sickness,
growing pale as that sheet she eats below:
no prayer can avert nor patron saint bless
away a hunger which in gorging grows,
lust for lifeforce flowing from her unrest.

As a swine she wings from grave's putrid clutch,
up to St. Stephen's, ringing doleful bells
whose tones inflect disease's noxious touch,
pestilence brewing in cistern & well
as rats flee her squeals in writhing bunches.

Too late kinsfolk pretend to lament her
memory, weeping as they disinter
her body from its deep worm-riddled berth,
hoping hint of their ailment to infer
by her cadaver's great gauntness or girth.

See! She has consumed her burial pall,
feasting fat now on her own flesh & blood!
Her own guts she chews, her own bile & gall,
limbs gnawed to bare bone & lips smeared by rud
of a banquet which would a ghoul appall.

Through her jaw a shaft of ashwood driven,
head clean from her shoulders then rudely cleft.
Again she claims what life is her given:
all her kindred fall dead, of blood bereft.
By livid lightning heaven is riven.

The Path of Grey

Adam Bolivar

I tread upon the Path of Grey—
    How long I have, I cannot say;
Above a wheel of ravens play,
    To taunt their tempting pleasing prey.

Cast out of Heaven and from Hell,
    I wander on and on;
I have no name I care to say,
    But if I must, I'm John.

In past I've walked on tracks of oak,
    Through grassy moor and fen;
And now on trains with stacks for smoke,
    I ride with ragged men.

Not good or bad, I walk the line,
    For borders are my home;
My loyalties may intertwine;
    In twilight e're I roam.

I dwell in shadows and in fears,
    Which one dare not believe;
Cats arch their backs when my step nears—
    A ghost on Hallow's Eve.

Semblance

David Barker

Remember how, in youth, I thought I saw
A scene unfolding far from Earth's blue sphere
Out on the rim, where Yuggoth reigns in fear,
A vision or mad dream that left me raw?
Upon a plane was laid an altar stone
Encircled by a tribe of wasplike things
Performing rites on one held down by rings
Of gold so tight, they pierced through flesh to bone.

But was it mere illusion, or much more—
Perhaps a glimpse beyond the mundane veil?
This memory's a thing that I abhor;
I pity one so young whom fiends assail.
His callow face, it quite familiar seems,
Like one I've glimpsed in mirrors in my dreams!

Inspired by H. P. Lovecraft's sonnet
"IV. Recognition" in *Fungi from Yuggoth.*

A Creature of the Twilight

Wade German

You ask me of that skull beneath the glass;
Each curio displayed here tells a tale,
But this one speaks of lore from elder time.
Once, when I traveled through the world of men
To search out sages (if true sages were),
I met a madman on the ancient road,
Whose aspect, and wild eyes, at once conveyed
A mind that hoarded wisdom. Warily
He asked which route I went; I gave reply,
But this disturbed him visibly. He said
Mayhap the marks upon my map were wrong;
That one needs be on guard when gone that way.
I remember his voice and lecture well:
"It is a twilight realm, a haunted place
Forever marred by strange ensorcellments
Called down in times of witch wars, long ago.
Dark aftermath of magics radiate
Within the very soil, the dust, the stones,
And no good thing can grow there anymore.
No sunlight penetrates directly there,
And evening never draws full darkness down;
It is a zone of half-light and half-dark,
The gloaming field of dead decaying dream.
A host of roaming mutant horrors prey
On those who cross its blasted, cratered scape;

And revenants of charnel lairs arise
To follow those who tread too near their tombs.
Do you not know the legend of the land?
A dark cathedral city lies out there
Necropolis-like, a mouldered ruin now.
Though ground down by the gnawing tooth of time,
Its sprawling mass of masonries remain
Enough to tell how great their builders were,
How little we. Over the rubble piles,
The shattered towers, walls, the broken domes
Of temples carved by artifice antique
(All looted now, if treasure you would seek),
Unnatural auroras haunt the skies
Like spectral sentinels, of shifting hue . . .
That realm was steeped in ancient sorceries,
Where magi had assumed a noble class.
Who knows if it was one, or many leagued
That first unsphered the spirits from what worlds
Removed in astral darks; but they arrived
With alien sciences occult and old,
Become as viziers to the courts and thrones
Of theocratic creatures power-bent,
Who governed cults of lucre, lust and vice.
That was an age of evil renaissance:
Dark revelations flowered through the fields

Of physics, metaphysics, psychic arts,
While braziers for a thousand idols burned . . .
They waxed as gods for centuries, then waned
Into a deep decline and decadence:
Divisions led to strife betwixt their sects;
Within the sects themselves, and schisms spread
Even as warlocks called down total war:
With artifacts of rare, arcane device,
They warped the weather, scorched the living sky,
Causing the clouds to rain a silver ash
That turned to crimson as it touched the earth.
Any exposed to that dread substance died;
All others atomized as flashing winds
Blasted the blinded air with Hell-born howls . . .
And demons allied to those theocrats
Inhabit still the ruins . . ."
                         Here he paused,
His countenance turned blank, as one immersed
In deep abstraction, turning over thought,
Muttering all the while but to himself,
Until his muttering grew wearisome,
And I had long since wearied on my way
Through all the human lands, now nearly home.
I thanked him for a fine intelligence

Then hacked him down by sword, and took his head,
As sage to sage this "creature" would converse,
To mine the ore of wisdom in his brain.
The vein did not run deep. I placed him here
When there was nothing more of which to speak.

Cometfall

DJ Tyrer

The stars were no different
Save for one single, singular change
A new star ablaze in the heavens
A bearded star of doom
A comet heading straight for Earth
Predictions were presented
Calculations were made
Contingencies confirmed
An announcement went out
Humanity would survive
Yes, it would be awful
The worst natural disaster ever
The Pacific fringes devastated
As it struck the peaceful ocean
But there was time to evacuate
Plenty of time to prepare
Unfortunately
Nobody factored in
It waking Cthulhu early

Candy Corn Caresses

Ashley Dioses

Her jack-o'-lantern grin gleams like the sprites
That lure like will-o'-wisps throughout the night.
Her hair of straw; what lovely yellow gold
Is spun atop her crown, that all behold.
Her lips are painted hues of orange and black
To conjure tastes of pumpkin spice, yet lack
My kisses pressed against to sample them.
Her button eyes invite like blackest gems.
When night should fall upon the Samhain lea,
My scarecrow love, my queen, awaits for me.
Her hand it beckons, yellow-orange, with white
Bespeckled fingertips that vow delight
In giving candy corn caresses, till
The dawn should rise and leave but autumn's chill.

The Garden of Night

Andrew White

In dreams where blood-red flowers grow,
The Mage in black makes midnight glow.
Foxes dance in mad array:
"Change is coming," they seem to say.
How long, how long until it ends?
Dirt grows cold and sky descends.
Whispers, whispers from the Earth—
The garden of night will soon give birth . . .

Inspired by Yoann Lossel's painting *The Whispering Garden*

Death Confession:
A Golden Shovel

LindaAnn LoSchiavo

It went awry, our lethal pact—but time
Brings no remorse. Planned suicide. Why does
One die while one survives? Unfairly, not
Unblest, I buried you and mourned yet bring
Dark spectral memories along. Relief
Ends when the noose of night unites dead you
And me. Expelled from light, your ghost haunts all
The same. Clairvoyants say, "Restless souls have
Questions." Confession: feigning death, I lied!

after Edna St. Vincent Millay

Communion

Manuel Pérez-Campos

A clan concurrence of exiguous cyclopean ammonite
delicately tentacled, gluttonous, hypersensitive

and encased in scarlet-striped shell armours
of logarithmic aragonite translucence palpitates

in prodigious aeonic aestivation encrusted (albeit
with spasmodic erasures and crushings)

in an exposed riparian stratum of pale micritic
limestone at Tepeyac as though in a funebrial

collective dream. They who knew themselves
axiomatic and the measure of all sediment-

hatched, riptide-borne, kelp-shadowed things
have arrived out of the early Campanian to convey

through feeling-tones that they are a tenacious
mutation, and that we are evolutionarily

entangled; and as I, beguiled by such strange
accueil, invite them to probe my psyche at will,

they attempt instead unmitigated reanimation
through appropriation of my vital energies—

until I sense them fidgeting starkly and about
to crawl: and as I open my mouth with unregulated

fear at the unstoppable imminence of becoming
undimensioned, each sucks my scream into itself.

The Witch's Tree

Jason Hardy

I burned down
The witch's tree.
I confess.
It was me.

It was eating
Another kid.
So I done
What I did.

I could see
Just his boots
Poking out
From the roots.

Trees are wood.
They can burn.
So I threw
My lantern.

It went up
Like a torch
While she sat
On her porch.

Then I just
Ran like hell
Before she could
Cast a spell.

She don't know
It was me
That burned down
Her damned tree.

Kids wear mask
On Halloween.
If you know
What I mean.

Don't tell her
What I done.
It's bad enough
I'm her son.

I burned down
The witch's tree
Before the next
Kid was me.

Last Soldier on the Beach

Jay Sturner

A man lies dying on a beach of burning smoke; one brave soldier among many. Gripped in hand: a photo of his fiancé. This he lets drop—his body is now a garden of wet, tattered roses. And despite his dimming sight, the world around him has yet to change, to reveal even a subtle flare of the next realm. The waiting is all too ordinary: screeching gulls, skittering crabs, sky the same earthly blue it has always been.

After time unmeasured he hears approaching footsteps in the sand. His head falls to the side knowingly—Death, working the beach, has come for him at last. But thoughts turn to what Death now means to him. This corrupt thing that smuggled so many of his friends out of their youth. He shakes his head in anger, red droplets smacking the sand.

Death emerges from the haze, a shapeless, distorted aspect of windblown smoke and fire. It transforms into something more substantial as it nears the soldier: billowing black cloak; gaunt face; stiff, exaggerated gait. The soldier scowls at the entity, harder than he ever did at the enemy. He begins to chuckle. Death suddenly strikes him as funny, this bony, somber cliché, the odd reality of it in front of his eyes. It shouldn't be here—not for him; not now.

The soldier reaches for his machine gun, cringing in pain. Screaming expletives, he lifts the gun and fires directly at the approaching form until the bullets run out. Death stops, turns, goes another way. Minutes pass. Then hours, days, a week. By now the soldier has bled out, his spirit tangled with stark fear and pain. Flies have laid eggs in several wounds; thoughts of their hatching plague his mind. Weeks go by. How many? Day and night, he remains alone.

Now we find the soldier picked clean by scavengers. The elements have done their scrubbing. All that remains are a half-buried skeleton, a crab nestled in each eye socket, and *consciousness*. From here the soldier sees Death begin its second approach. When it reaches him, Death lifts an arm and drops a loose handful of bullets. Each is an echoing ping against his skull. Before the soldier is led away, Death leans in with frigid breath and says, "Do not disrespect me again."

The Black Goat

Linn Donlon

We have been told her kingdom is a tomb,
A charnel house where mankind should not go;
Yet dimly from her dark and fearsome womb
I see a thousand thousand creatures flow.
I see her newborns batten on their kin,
Devouring their flesh in hungry greed;
It seems she does not view this as a sin,
Accepting that the losses serve their need.
Upon the trampled ground the priestess sits,
Among the fox and hare, the wolf and hind,
And sucks from one among her thousand teats
That milk which brings perception to the mind.
If only I did not so fear to sink
With beasts before her, I could kneel and drink.

Knowing the Dragon

Geoffrey Reiter

The dragon slumbers underneath your feet:
We fear not the unknown—the known we fear.
You cannot feel the wyrm's blood-bubbling heat:
The dragon slumbers underneath your feet.
The horror comes when, from the beaten street,
The beast bursts forth in flames that smolder near.
The dragon slumbers underneath your feet:
We fear not the unknown—the known we fear.

Battle against the Dark Lord

Jordan Zuniga

Skies to churn, darkness to dwell,
Shadows lurk, horrors swell,
In the land so charred to ash,
Where arrows fly, and swords would clash,
The mud to fling where corpses fall,
And death would meet us all.
His reign so fierce, his grasp would not yield,
His grip upon our life and the battlefield,
The sound of roars, and constant fears,
Where the clouds depart and the heavens clear,
To gaze upon the tyrant beast,
Who comes to dine and us, to feast?
"To arms, to arms, the dragons here!
Ready the arms, victory is near!"
The mark then hit, the screams of pain,
We fight again with heightened disdain,
Against the horrors of arrow and sword,
To defeat the reign of the shadow lord . . .

Spider

Don Webb

Who brushed me
like the shadow of a beautiful woman?
I was sleeping
in my perfect white linen world
And I felt the swift caress
like a shadow running
or the impression of a song
sung yesterday.

A single silken thread
across my chest—
What was she planning while I slept?

Antiquarian Research

David C. Kopaska-Merkel

It wasn't so much the cadaverous curator,
nor the restless stirring under his grimy coat,
not his penetrating, silent stare
punctuated by obscure ominosities,
they were nothing new, but you,
under glass, final scream still on your lips,
and the tome from which you'd read,
blood warm, squirming in my hands,
its many mouths snarling and spitting,
and the sound it made when I flung
it in the fire, gave me quite a turn.

A Little Song of Death

Carl E. Reed

When in the fullness of fast-flowing time
the joy of flesh becomes but ache & pain
nature succors & stops with death sublime
the manic antics of the Sons of Cain.
Rich wanton feast & wild, ribald song
strong wine & thighs—ecstatic poetry—
intoxicate the spirit; though ere long
the bell that tolled for others tolls for thee.
That thunder in the mountain: avalanche
of broken trees, & boulders, & black snow
rolls juggernaut downslope—no man can stanch
the final doom of **BOOMCRASH:** 'Way you go!
Madness, horror, brief joy, grief, red rage, strife—
berserk fast-fading visions: mordant life.

The Court of Azathoth

Ngo Binh Anh Khoa

I see the Daemon Sultan in my fever dream
And wondered how such horror could have come to be;
Much like a mass of tumors festering rapidly
Amid the heart of universes He does seem.

Around his slumbering body blare the maddening sounds
Of monotonous flutes—whose notes would form and rend
The fabrics of all Space and Time and never end—
Where every blasphemous monstrosity abounds?

To keep their mindless Lord imprisoned in His sleep,
All kinds of pandemonium, His courtiers wreak—
Wild bat-things dance, live fires rage, huge planets shriek,
And Chaos crawls before its Sire's pulsing heap.

The longer I am in this dream, the more I feel
Another piece of me gets crudely ripped apart
By those cursed flutes played by misshapen claws. My heart,
I fear, may burst. (If so, will I die here for real?)

Then, suddenly, the noises stop, the music dies,
And all those cosmic beings, silenced, bow their heads
Before their stirring Master's roars; each rumble shreds
A Universe into nonexistence. His great eyes

Soon open. One by one the Outer Gods then fade,
Absorbed into the void that from His waking forms.
The Sultan's breaths become apocalyptic storms
That raze what's left till every World has been unmade.

I scream awake and find myself still in one piece;
So is the world—the sky, the earth, each breeze-stirred plant,
And people minding their own business. Still, I can't
Stop wondering when He will be roused, and Life shall cease.

Destiny

David Schembri

When you lie in shadows,
Fretting in your bed,
Don't you shed a tear for me;
I *choose* to fight the dead.

When you run through tunnels,
Hiding in the gloom,
Fear not when I don't follow,
The dark is my playroom.

I cried and hid when I was young,
So many years ago;
Zombies ate my parents' whole,
I watched them die so slow.

Raised in hidden valleys deep,
Within the mud and cold,
Forging clothes from beasts I'd slain,
Eyes wild until I'm old.

Earth is lost in ruin now,
Stolen by the dead;
They rose from graves and marched the towns,
To paint our streets blood red.

I'm clad in armored leathers,
With gauntlets strong and true;
My spear and sword and firearm,
I'm here! So rest anew.

Call me and you'll find me there,
Scream! And I'll come your way,
To fling you right behind me,
To have you live this day.

So when you're safe and sound at home,
Nestled in your bed,
Never waste your tears for me;
I *choose* to fight the dead.

A Song of Two Deaths

Ian Futter

The solitary crow,
with rattling shriek,
screams out his sad song
from cold carrion beak,

While the warm winter breeze
breathes his call through the fog
past the corpse-cluttered carnage
of the Bandar-log.

With clawing and ripping,
The snarl and the bite;
the mad monkey people
eternally fight,

but break, for a moment,
from their murderous purge
to mark the sad sounds
of funereal dirge,

which tells of a father
and a friendship; both past:
a screech through the silence;
despondent and ghast.

All the vampires cease sucking
and the ghouls halt their feed,
repelled from rank meals
by the cries that they heed.

And the spectres all shiver
and the creatures all cower
at the heart breaking herald,
with his message so dour.

Still the crow carries on
with his story of loss,
while the banshees in horror
stuff their ears with grave moss,

But the song won't be silenced,
till the story is heard,
and all terror still trembles
at the sound of this bird.

Flower of Evil

Manuel Arenas

On the tree of life, I am but a bitter fruit,
Acrid to the palate and oppressive to the senses.
In the societal garden I am a blight.
Not even the worms of the earth dare partake of my flesh.
A vampiric weed, I suckle life from my peers,
shunning the light of day to grow hatefully in the dark.
Although I am alone, no wallflower am I,
but a flower of evil: for all those that touch me—die!

Nordic Instinct

Charles Lovecraft

Adventure-prone, the maddened clang of swords
And bashing balls with spikes that thud on helms;
The weedy wash of rushing main that whelms
The senses in the salt-sea spray, affords
New shores of blazing, promised victories,
And spoils as nameless as their countlessness.
Norse raiders rode their logic to suppress
The foe and vanquish their eternities.
Survival was instinctive truth to them,
As if Crom was the fittest god of all,
Who would instruct the very sword that thirsts
And gluts its sharp-edged tongue in frenzied whim;
Or, keening singing its deep song of thrall—
Explodes the chains with flexing muscle bursts!

The Lady in the Wood

Geoffrey Reiter

He traveled toward the lonesome wood
Beyond the gardens and the glades.
Upon a high place then he stood,
Looked down where winter snows in flood
Melt off in liquid braids.

Descending to the valley, he
Returned into that gloomy green
And found the path that wound through tree
And shrub, the human highway, free
Inside the sylvan scene.

He saw the lady on the road.
She wore a dress of blue brocade
That from her fulsome figure flowed
Beneath a belt of brown, and showed
Her shoulders unafraid.

He did not move, but yet she turned
And looked on him with diamond eyes
That gleamed in shards of sun, and burned
Like ice on flesh, a gaze that churned
The air in wild surmise.

She spoke sweet words in lilting tone,
A song that swelled, like pulpy fruit,

Enticing, lyrical, a moan
Meandering in a tongue unknown,
Melodious as a lute.

He took her in embrace and kissed
Those rich red lips that late had sung
Their faerie song; she took his wrist
Within her slender grasp to tryst
Him toward the elm, where clung

The vining ivy twined around
The coarse grey trunk. Her lips, they oped
To sheen-white teeth. Without a sound
They slithered, slunk down to the ground.
Her pall-pale fingers groped

Into the small of his broad back.
And then his own great jaws gaped wide:
He bared his fierce fangs in attack,
His flesh convulsed in hunger's wrack,
As hellishly he cried

And brought his teeth down toward her throat.
Yet then, she rolled upon the path
From out his grasp. A piping note

Of glee escaped her lips afloat
The air, as in her wrath

She proffered then the silver blade
Concealed within her graceful gown.
Her blue-clad arm, in silk arrayed,
Arced through the shadows and the shade
And struck the monster down.

And so, eyes wide, his clean-shorn head
Rolled toward the margin of the road
As from his sundered neck was shed
The stolen blood, which now outspread
In rivulets that flowed

Into the thirsty earth. And she,
The lady in the wood, then smiled
And cleaned and sheathed her sword, now free
To head for home, once more to see
Her husband and her child.

In the Beginning

Melissa Ridley Elmes

In the beginning was a void
and then the stars came,
taking their places onstage
behind the velvet curtain, waiting
for the signal that the show begins
in the vast galaxy theater.
As if by cue, facing the empty expanse,
one shimmering star opened her mouth
and sang one long, true note,
held for an infinity, sustained and sweet,
resonating and reverberating through
the darkness, the first note in the
music of the spheres. One by one
the other stars in turn added
their voices in variation, joining
bright descant to that first clear note,
filling space and time with starsong.
They sang the planets into being, and
the comets, and all the things of sky
and ocean and earth. Atmospheres
hummed into existence, and interstellar
galaxies, and the chorus went on and on,
their performance achingly lovely and
unceasing, filling eternal emptinesses
with encore, after encore, after encore.

In Her Defence

Claire Smith

1.

Bullies nickname her: *Vixen!*
when she blushes at older boys
when they pinch her backside.
They style her hair, brimmed

with silly-string: orange, pink, white.
School-gates like dungeon doors:
slammed shut, chained and bolted.
While teacher-guards patrol endless

corridors; they threaten lip with a visit
to the Head; and govern routes of weekly
cross-country runs. An autumn morning,
drizzle hangs in the air; she lags behind

with the smokers and the drinkers.
Skulks back along the canal towpath,
skirts the edge of dim-lit woods . . .
She finds a lock-keeper's cottage

with its open window and promises.

2.

The open window is in easy reach. Layers
of spiderwebs form a dusty barrier.
So she scrambles through, knocks

over a dinner-pan tower. They clatter
onto the ground. The stench of rank
curry slaps her across the face.

Plates are scattered over the tiled floor
as if someone has had a temper fit.
In the front room she finds chairs,

cushions empty; cracked bones
of legs and backs gnawed
by starved dogs. The bedrooms, bare,

except mattresses, and bedbugs
layered in decayed eiderdowns.

3.

She falls asleep among the shadows;
coloured overlapping cubes: greens,
blues, crimson flashes; curtains
wave together. Wardrobe doors

swing, drawers clang; bumps,
clatters from window-frames
as night shades over day,

clings to the sun and forces it
down below the tips of trees
below hedgerows,
below the horizon.

By What Right Do You Call Yourself Patience?

Thomas Goff

> She sat like Patience on a monument,
> Smiling at grief.
>
> —*Twelfth Night*

Grievers and priests adore you, my cold éclair,
You and your chastely seducing marble dimples.
Compliant lip-curves emit upon listless air
Forbearance like foam, you've swallowed so many simples.
Your face, all your stone exoskeleton chapped,
Rain-chafed, yet still you sit in wait to hatch
A coffin, hoping the old green corpse has napped,
No more: a livid cadaver-life you'd snatch,
Hoping the chick-like lich pecks its way out.
What Maestro lofts the baton for his next ictus?
You are not Patience, carcasses are. Grave clouts
Lift, peeling away skin, mold, rot. Desecration's
Indifferent to them, and they to you, so-called Patience.
Cherubic lips loosen, Time carves the abyss-dark rictus.

Incubus

Scott J. Couturier

Your succulent weight
compresses my thigh—
crushing plight
of lust as you writhe,
groan & gorge.

I harden—you harden.
Daemonic eyes bore
my sick bliss into dross.
You suck it out, give
back loss.

Your breath reeks of
semen & sweat-stain—
of tumescent eternities spent
in coital anonymity,
oily taint.

Thrust—gasp. Reel &
roil, pitch & moan.
A web of dusk robes
your groin, drapes
your grin.

I scream—wail to voids
of no caring. You kiss
my mouth with crescents
of fire, suckle blood from
baying lips.

Then—greed slaked—gone.
Gone to darkness cradling
your swollen appetites. Alone,
I reel in insatiate terror,
in need.

Heolstor

Adam Bolivar

Unholy Heolstor,   in Hel an earl,
An occult ettin,   offspring of Night,
Dark and doomful,   dreadful to behold,
Haunted the heath,   hated by folk,
Flaying flesh from   fools who crossed him,
Their strident screams   resounding afar,
A weighty warning   the wise heeded.
Cyndraca was called,   a cunning man,
Whose sword had slain   several ettins,
His feats famous   far and wide.
On his way, a wizard,   one-eyed and hoary,
Lent him a lantern   laden with runes
To drive out the darkness   bedevilling the land.
Cyndraca came   to the cold heath,
Murky and moist,   mist swirling,
Holding high   the hallowed lamp,
To find his foe   flat in the gorse,
Sleeping unseen,   obscured by a cloak,
But the lantern's light   laid him bare.
Quickly Cyndraca   killed Heolstor,
Hewing the head   of the horrid ettin,
Whose black blood   bathed his sword.
Cyndraca kept   the cloak of Night,
A blessing in battle,   and a boon to thieves.

Cast

Ron L. Johnson II

My reflection reaches out for me
The image I cast sees more than me
My shadow wants to harm me too
But I defuse the light to kill the shadow that knew

All time can seem far away and dark
The cuttlefish blends in to conceal its mark
When my mind's eye only looks outward and stark
The sky starts to shatter apart and that's when
My reflection starts to maniacally grin

Phantasms

Wade German

They come sometimes at eventide,
　　The apparitions just appear;
From mist and moonlight streams they glide,
　　Out of some otherworldly sphere.

In aspects fair, or grim and gaunt,
　　Composed of cobwebs they all seem;
They do no harm but only haunt,
　　Strange as impressions shaped in dream.

Their stays are brief, but quite intense.
　　And when the spectres visit me,
As if by some uncanny sense
　　I understand they strive to be—

Whether as figments mind-conceived
　　Or visitants by limbo sent—
And know their being is achieved
　　When they have reached their vanishment.

The Seeker's Lament
(a villanelle)

Frank Coffman

I yearn to *dream* a place where all is bright,
The darkness shattered by a strong dawn sun,
But nightmares show a place of Endless Night.

I long to glimpse these glowering stars take flight,
Fleeing—before the great Day-Star to run.
I seek—*in dreams*—a place where all is bright.

In trance, in sleep, I delve the Sky's great height,
Looking for gleaming *Hope*—but I find none.
My night terrors travel to Eternal Night.

I know now that deliverance' chance is slight—
Knew it as soon as these visions had begun!—
My wakings too find no place were all is bright.

Must I resolve myself to this sad plight?
Can this wretched *Darkness* never be undone?
Can I escape this land of Endless Night?

Nay! Since I spoke those words—a Forbidden Rite!
The Gate is open! Demon wights have come—and won!
Though I might seek a place where all is bright,
These Night Wraiths *Real!* I'm doomed to Endless Night!

A Crime of Passion

G. O. Clark

Look closely
at her eye, the dark iris,
that clock face pinned
dead center,

minute and hour hands
precisely stopped at midnight.

Listen intently
to her silent heart, that cold
absence of ticking,
pulse dead,

flow of blood slowed to nothing;
seat of emotions empty.

Step back
and see the bloody hammer
swung in anger in your
trembling hand,

it's claw-end incapable
of undoing one's raging passion.

On the Fantasque Ballet Premiere of *Afternoon of a Faun*

Manuel Pérez-Campos

Humor the naked ecstasy of the great danger
dancer Nijinsky: humor his laurel-freighted
pointed ears and piebald thighs as he, an acolyte
of the maenads, eschews prudery and the guilt-
bound pallor with open hand next to his phallus
in this frieze dream of antiquity come to life
through a spell out of asphodel dimnesses built.
Released for your delectation here in Paris,
he keeps dream-ground under him like a hexameter
on the threshold of an epic as with subdued
twirls he haunts a gauze-swathed sylph who must stay aloof
under Selene's counsel by retreating in light
en pointe whilst reaching out to him. And as he hunkers
in imagined solitude, resigned to surcease,
and presses to his loins her dropped scarf, there come murmurs
lost to him, as though from beneath the roots of trees.

Yethwood

Oliver Smith

In Yethwood on the granite hill,
as winter's coming on,
the Wisht-Hounds and Herlathing cry,
their dreadful hunting song.
Three untrue lords came riding fast
upon the frost-white road,
as the snow fell ever faster
down; frozen, deep, and cold.

In Yethwood by an ancient keep
a warhorse ran unchained;
hooves hammered in the icy night
beside the frozen stream
In a grove of oaks, that crouched, low
like waiting thieves, three lords
were caught; as in the distance, loud
the golden trumpets roared.

The hour had passed, their battle lost;
for victory, drums beat,
Their king threw them down in anger.
The Yethwood branches creaked
beneath the weight of unknown fruit,
hung high upon the tree,
until, upon the moss they spilled
their bloody pith and seed.

Yet a new king called them, to come
through darkly purpling night.
In the thicket, King Herla stood
beyond the cold moonlight.
In his hair of green, grew ivy;
his crown was mistletoe.
Three untrue lords with broken swords
bent down before his throne.

"Knights, saddle up!" their master cried
and "Ride, Herlathing, ride!"
Away galloped that dreaded king,
with three lords at his side.
Three dead lords with broken swords;
frost threaded in their bones.
Three dead lords who forever ride
beyond the frozen road.

Three lords in Sunlight-Never-More.
No more to fight and feast.
Three untrue lords no never more
above the ground to sleep.
Never do the conspirator's rest,
above the earth they ride;
the Yethwood Knights all screaming
at dead king Herla's side.

With his hellish dogs all howling
around the wood they fly,
and chase the mad, wandering moon
across the stormy sky.
The Wisht-Hounds and Herlathing cry,
their dreadful hunting song,
in Yethwood, on the granite hill,
as winter's coming on.

Whalesong

DJ Tyrer

Scientists finally learn to translate
Word analogues of the whalesong
Unlock the messages it contains
Much as expected they find:
Love songs
Declarations of strength
Invitations
Greetings
But then one is found
Repeated over and over
That doesn't fit the trend
A warning
"It is rising! It is rising!"
Then, "The End of All Things comes!"

Dusk

Andrew White

Moths appear when dusk arrives,
The time of day when magic thrives.
The last of the sun meets the rising moon,
Spirits will be dancing soon.

The glow of dusk on her tattooed skin
Hints that something is about to begin.
Mystical energies are bursting through,
A timeless ritual starts anew.

Nativity

David Barker

The thing spoke not, but in my mind I heard
A call to soar through vast domains of space
To where I might engage with his fey race,
But sanctity of soul was not assured.
"Through sunset's rose-hued portal . . ."—then a word
Unknown to me, but judging from his face
I knew it meant we'd visit that strange place
To which my instinct pled "Do not be lured!"

Below us swept an endless city, strange,
Its towers rising high to purple clouds.
Around the base of each were swarming crowds
Whose mantic hum my brain would soon derange.
"No more," I cried. "Return me to my home."
"I have," he hissed. "'Tis there beneath the dome!"

Inspired by H. P. Lovecraft's sonnet
"V. Homecoming" in *Fungi From Yuggoth.*

Blindsight

Lori R. Lopez

Wanly complected, ethereal of body. The stuff of clouds.
They were right, the Spiritualists with their spooky sessions.
What's the word? Séances. Language is less defined now.
Wispy as form. My thinking fluid like the rest of me,
composed of vapor. Life so brief, why all the fuss? In the end
we are the same. Our flesh unpeeled layer by layer.
Falling in flakes resembling snow; melted by grave or fire.

It comes down to this. Mere shades of who we are.
Correction, were. Even alive there was little to separate,
distinguish, but imagination. Ideas we shaped or chose to
accept, become. It was really about that, inspiring our deeds.
Building fences, breaking them down. Herded or left to
wander alone. What did any of it mean or matter?
In the end we dissolve to specters—spectators . . .

Ghosts of ourselves, watching both Present and Past.
Spirits once possessed for adventure, romance, beauty,
whimsy, art, the dark, mayhem. Released to bear witness—
behold the misery, examine the missteps of Skins
with their fleeting beating hearts and emotions!
In hindsight or blindsight, waiting to view what happens
when dust settles, pages turn, wheels of Progress churn.

Breathless, we anticipate the next Chapter, Act, Scene
of this play on Life and Death. It was all so serious,
yet we took it too lightly. Ignored the bleats of
Philosophers and Sheep like we were immune, immortal.
The Lambs knew what we did not, that each moment
was precious. Each drop of existence pure joy.
They frolicked and laughed . . . until we killed them.

The irony is, in Death as in Sleep our eternal task
remains to count them. Over and over. Because they do.
They always did. Every. Single. Life.
Those who couldn't peer through the fog of untruths
before their time expired, destined to study and take
stock . . . tally each victim of oppression, injustice.
Whether human or not. They had feelings too.

They were not so different inside. At last we see.

Bold Voyager

Darrell Schweitzer

So the demon bore me up in my dream
beneath an ash-gray sky
and set me down on a beach of bare stone
beside a waveless sea.
I said, "I will cross that sea."
"No one ever has," the demon replied.
"Is it death then?"
"Oh, no," said the demon,
"The Styx is the most traveled of all waters,
  and Lethe the most yearned for.
  It is easy to reach both of those.
  This is the Abyss, which has no farther shore,
  where darkness yawns beyond the last extinct stars,
  beyond the last rolling, black planets,
  beyond even the throne of Azathoth,
  and the void is utterly silent and truly infinite."
  Nevertheless, I gathered such detritus as I found
  along the water's edge, fashioned a craft,
  and set out.
"Bold voyager," the demon whispered,
"Very soon you shall yearn for the Styx,
  and thirst desperately for Lethe."

The Daemon Lord

Chad Hensley

My sword is drawn, black helmet shields my face.
White laser beams shoot from my day-glow eyes
As daemons burned, they melted into space.
A six-winged form flew out of sunken skies

With human arms attached to swollen hooks.
A head of tentacles with mouths did thrash
And moan as massive bloated belly shook;
A hundred puckered holes with fangs did gnash.

I took a deep breath and backwards I stepped,
Observing the daemon's great enormous girth.

When from far shadows, something spiderlike crept—
A six-foot walking womb bursts gore with birth:

A cavernous mouth with stalactite teeth
On giant centipede-like legs beneath.

Eye of Sapphire, Eye of Emerald

Kurt Newton

It once was a place of sacred devotion,
a temple in the clouds,
until a desperate young woman appeared
clutching an odd-eyed cat.

She said a dangerous man was after her,
there were bruises on her neck and arms.
The monks conferred and granted asylum,
even though women were strictly forbidden.

Respectfully, she kept to herself,
spending long hours in the stone garden.
The dangerous man never came,
the cat her only companion.

She died shortly thereafter,
a death as mysterious as her arrival.
The cat looked on as the monks buried her
in the spot where she was most at peace.

For days the feline sat on her grave,
as still as the surrounding statuary.
Eyes closed it appeared to contemplate
its place in the universe.

When the cat at last opened its eyes,
their colors had traded places.
The monks, believing in miracles,
began to worship it like a deity.

The cat was given the Emperor's Chair,
fresh fish daily from the gorge,
a mouse on a string for exercise,
crickets for desert.

The monks groomed the cat's coat
until it was as smooth as satin,
kept its claws sharp as razors,
its long whiskers waxed.

Chants were written to commemorate
the arrival of the odd-eyed deity.
Mosaics created, statues carved
for he who had no name.

The cat barely acknowledged them,
napping during daylight hours.
At night, it would prowl the temple,
its feet silent in the candelit dark.

But suspicions quickly spread

when the monks began to die in their sleep.
One by one they were found wide-eyed,
pale as ghosts, mouth agape.

There must be a murderer among them.
Several were accused, one condemned
to walk the narrow Ledge of Truth.
The monk fell into the gorge below.

But the mysterious deaths continued
and eyes soon turned toward the cat.
It was decided the cursed feline
was to be banished from the temple.

But several zealous disciples
struck as the deadline approached,
killing all who voted against
the embodiment of their worship.

The remaining monks died virtuous
alone, aghast, in their sleep,
the cat now the only occupant
of the once sacred temple.

The feline returned to the stone garden,
to the spot where the woman was buried.

It sat, head raised, eyes closed
as if posing for one its statues.

Months later, the temple was visited
by a monk returning from a quest.
The madness that had gripped the religious order
was too egregious to overcome.

The temple was left to the elements
and the inevitable ravages of time.
It is rumored there is an odd-eyed cat
that haunts it to this day.

Survive against the Swarm

Jordan Zuniga

Mud to splatter, blood to flow,
Sound of steel, "Onward ho!"
Battle against the nightmarish creatures,
Slaughter those with horrid features!
Wrap, entangle, then to thrash!
Steel to meet as blood would splash!

"Cover your own, they swarm in spite!
Lest we die in the darkness of the night!"
Arrows mustered, shields then drawn,
To survive for the break of dawn.

Circle, push, endless number,
Tear apart, torn asunder,
Light to draw, the battle won,
Nightmares defeated by the touch of the sun.

Elizabeth Siddal Rossetti, Cemetery Superstar

LindaAnn LoSchiavo

Retaining fame one hundred sixty years
After I died *unknown*—artwork unsold,
My verses unpublished—has been bizarre.
Do stars need darkness to appreciate
Their glowing? Or wise men to point them out?

My temperamental husband, mad with guilt,
Laid me to rest with poems, his bound book.
This he missed—more than my companionship.
Where's *my* work now? Just then there came a crash.

Rude crowbars pried apart my long-sealed lid.
Men open-mouthed like choristers stared shocked.

Distraught, he'd sent them. *Dig her up!* He'll learn
My flesh looked pale, my red hair's grown more wild.

Rossetti's poems sweetened maggots' meals.
Worm-eaten scraps had crowned my coffined head,
A spectral tapestry akin to my
Ophelia pose, a dead girl prettified,
Myself a teen when painted by Millais.
A painting's fame forgets dead models—but
Art helps us dream back everything that's lost.

Blackburn's Bloom

Manuel Arenas

There is a graveyard on the outskirts of the forsaken settlement of
Morelville, in Western Massachusetts, which is attached to an ancient
chapel that fell into some disrepute sometime around 19— when the
vicar, Eldred Blackburn, was found to be dabbling in the dark arts. This
was ascertained when a local tramp named Doran stopped the sexton,
Merritt Fosser, while making his rounds in the churchyard, to tell him
he had espied the vicar skulking about the potter's field nightly, in a
ghoulish mesonoxian routine.

Determined to unearth the truth, the sexton returned to the
boneyard with the tramp in the midnight hour. To keep him from
blundering onto the scene and ruining any element of surprise, he
enjoined Doran to stay behind the gate whilst he took cover amongst the
neglected tombstones of the uncherished dead and waited for the
questionable clergyman to make his entrance to the grounds. In short
time he saw, to his horror and profound disenchantment, what he had
honestly hoped not to see. There, genuflecting in front of an open grave,
was the wiry form of Blackburn, silhouetted in the full moonlight,
declaiming blasphemous litanies from a black girdle book, and pouring
blood from the Eucharistic chalice onto a darksome kernel he had
deposited in the tainted soil environing the godforsaken remains of the
adjacent occupiers. When confronted, the vicar drew a billhook from his
cassock and set upon the sexton with wanton fury. Doran, overhearing
the kerfuffle, ran to the sexton's aid and wrested the blade from
Blackburn's hand, but not before the perfidious vicar landed a fatal blow
on Fosser's temple, causing him to bleed out into the tainted soil.

The parishioners paid for Fosser's burial, then summarily abandoned the church, which had been vitiated by the damnable affair. Blackburn was deposed and lived out the rest of his days in seclusion as a pariah, allegedly continuing in his shadowy pursuits, and when he finally relinquished his mortal coil he was interred in the same ground on which he had performed his profane ritual. Doran became an unlikely folk hero and, for a pint of ale, would regale his benefactors with a hair-raising account of his part in that dreadful night with a phantasmagorical epilogue telling of how on the All Hallow's Eve following his interment, Blackburn rose from his uneasy rest in the potter's field and attempted to enter the sacred soil of the graveyard proper, but the sentinel soul of Merritt Fosser refused him entry. Purportedly, they argued at the lychgate until the cockcrow when Blackburn's curst soul was compelled to return to his infernal reward. His corrupted body, however, collapsed where it stood and was found the following day sprawled by the gate, where it was retrieved and replaced in its grave with an ash wood stake driven through the heart to keep it from rising again. They say Fosser's soul continues to play the role of sentinel, keeping the likes of the wicked vicar away from the consecrated ground.

On a parting note, it is rumored that on Blackburn's cursèd burial plot there grew a prodigious flower of unholy provenance that thrived in moonlight and subsisted on vermin and whatever ghastly morsels lay within reach of its grasping roots from the neighboring graves. Its florets allegedly suggested a Death's-Head and if one were foolish enough to approach it, it would whisper vile malisons to curdle the blood and vex the soul. Nevertheless, to this day, if one is brave enough to traverse the overgrown and crumbling graveyard in the dead of night, one might still hear the baneful blossom trilling a paean to Hecate in its eldritch voice, and if one were to perhaps feed it a drop or two of blood, it might even see fit to divulge a secret from beyond the loury veil. Just beware if it comes to crave the taste.

Essential Guide to the Land of Dream

David C. Kopaska-Merkel

It begins with a door
of heavy blackened oak,
hinges of brass and brassy inlays
intricate, disturbing,
fanciful, we hope,
mantled in corrosion,
that mercifully obscures
features you fear to discern.
We were there already.

Beyond the door are steps
descending, uncounted (we've tried);
to either side, a vast echoic void,
filled with indescribable sounds;
one is grateful for the dark.
After descending for an immeasurable time,
one encounters the skeletal tops of trees
whose branches move discordantly;
there is no wind.
At last the stair ends in the soft black loam
of the unquiet forest, from which sprout
toadstools, beslimed and phosphorescent.
We were there already.

*   *   *

Away among the trees,
the toadstools grow hideously large;
they seem to sway, and some, to murmur;
this is vastly preferable
to the shapes one sometimes sees,
but never hears,
gliding among the farther trees:
pray that none approach!
but this is why you have brought
the packet of aromatic herbs
(you did, didn't you); their pungency
should be all you can smell
until you are disgorged
on to the rocky plain of Gha'at.
We were there already.

There may, in the distance,
be a village—avoid it.
Move quickly here,
for the village surely will;
its conical huts of bone,
scale, and thorn
are larger than they appear.
If you find yourself in a grassland,

move swifter yet; those creatures
that some call the cats of Belaar
prefer larger game,
but if that prove too fleet, you will do.
We were there already.

If somehow a road finds you,
take it,
but here you must move
swiftest of all,
and do not rest or tarry.
The road may convey you to a city,
enter there: you have almost reached
your destination, whatever it may be.
Beware the Dhole;
no need to travel swiftly now,
not speed nor herb will aid you
if you meet that pallid bulk,
abristle with fell tines,
and writhing tendrils, sinewy and agape,
in a dark and lonely street.
We were there already.

Watch and Wait

Margaret Curtis

Block out the signs today of the damned plague!
Reach out and shut the window, lock the door,
Turn deaf ears to the crowd now in a rage,
And count each can or bottle in your store.

Incessant rain pelts down, a thrumming tap.
The wind whips round your house, up through the floor,
While summer storms prize open every gap,
That you might better hear the creatures roar.

More loudly now than any other night,
The figments clash and clang along your street.
Their haggard, famished faces bear the blight.
They test your gate, a sharp persistent beat.

You dim the light, but you have smelled and seen
The bloody stench, and past the storm you hear
That somewhere up the road, beasts more obscene
Take now the lives of those you once held dear.

Time passes and the rattling sounds abate.
You take a risk and turn your Screen up bright.
Now "Watch and Act" they say, or is it "Wait"?
Could Waiting still or Acting now be right?

You listen, as you have done for so long,
For some clear path: stay safe or take a stand?
And who would come to aid you if you're wrong,
And you, yourself, become the screeching Damned?

You fall to silence as you always do.
These last of days—too many and too few!

The Ghosts' Autumnal Fair

Ngo Binh Anh Khoa

The full moon casts a web of silver
Below, where naked branches shiver,
And wind-stirred leaves all, murmuring, quiver
Amid the thickened mist; no sliver
Of warmth is present in the air;
Those spectral threads from heaven shed,
Like puppet strings, on tombstones spread
And raise the spirits of the dead
When comes the Ghosts' Autumnal Fair.

The graveyard's silence soon is broken
By utterances quietly spoken
Between the shades by moonbeams woken;
A whirlwind wild, their sights betoken.
They gracefully glide across the air;
Soft squeaks from out the swaying trees
And hoots midst rustling canopies
Join the nocturnal melodies
When comes the Ghosts' Autumnal Fair.

Figures from eras past and present—
With royals, nobles, slaves and peasants—
There mingle midst the luminescence
Of moon and stars strewn on the heavens
While distant wolf-songs fill the air—
A show of strange, breathtaking fashion;

If not for their complexion ashen,
Who'd think they're specters with such passion
When comes the Ghosts' Autumnal Fair.

Between the lofty and the lowly,
There's no division; all are wholly
Equal; their every mortal folly,
And worldly want, and vice unholy
Have long dispersed like dust midair.
Once all their vital breaths were spent,
And bodies 'neath the soil were sent,
All earthly ties they'd weaved were rent.
Only in Death are all things fair.

They dance on, fervently performing
From movements slow to paces storming
Throughout the night until the morning
In celebration—and in mourning;
Nostalgia haunts the silenced air.
The chill dissolves as light shines on
The graveyard at the break of dawn;
The trees are still, the dancers gone—
Until the next Autumnal Fair.

Churchyard Passacaglia

Thomas Goff

Tonight is for the gathering
Of souls that slither insect-like,
From under coffins' underwing-
Thin lids; up by tomb-crack turnpikes.

Tonight is for the gathering.

This night allows new freedom for
Half-airy, half-liquescent souls
Of high-rise cube or cabin floor;
Their lifetime dooms, grave-narrow holes.

Tonight is for the gathering.

The night air magnifies black bats'
Reconnaissance for souls and ghouls
Of note, in death deemed merest gnats.
Dark squadrons reap, heap, life-rich fools.

Tonight is for the gathering.

This night's a night for harvesting.
These ring-round-dancers can absorb
—Not bite, with mindless zombie-sting—
Fresh souls in one huge boneyard corb.

Tonight is for the gathering.

These midnight church bells, twelve in all,
Peal night's peak merriment, echoing
The amorous chant for souls who fall
To Satan's mess, though they still sing.

Deep midnight caps the gathering.

Those feasting now turn feasted-on,
Soul-scapegoats lodged in blood and molt
Must be devoured before the dawn;
What demons eat they're forced to bolt.

Past midnight goes the gathering.

Subside now, night chimes' echoing;
Salacious fiddle-music; flings
Of hand to new ghoul-partnerings;
The wish to cling, forevering:

Submit to first-light silencing.

Too late now for more gathering.

Fat Man and Yellow-Eyes: A Ghoulish Tale

Carl E. Reed

I met a ghoul of yellow eyes
    & protruding, rat-like teeth
feasting in the catacombs
    that warped & woofed beneath

the stately old ancestral home
    that long buried its dead
in ornate coffins sealed against
    the haunting, gnawing dread

of daggered fingernails prying up
    what tradesmen hammered shut
to keening bleatings of feckless priests
    of manicured, perfumed cut.

"Fiend!" cried I. "Foul cannibal!
    Eater of necrotic flesh!
You dare make meal of beloved kin
    interred for eternal rest?"

Yellow-Eyes snickered, prehensile snout
    matted with fatty gore:
"I should let such rich meat go to waste?
    I think not! Bring me more!

You lecture me, fat carnivore?
    Have you never paused to wonder
why family forbids its undertakers
    from embalming those who blunder

across the river Styx to regions
    forever lost to light:
realms infernal, dark eternal
    devouring, rabid night?"

I turned & fled, mocking laughter
    ringing in my ears,
hot blood surging in my veins
    taking counsel of my fears

I hobble-bopped away as fast
    as girth & breath would let
my frigid soul, grown old & cold
    fair-shriveled at the threat

of ghoulish implication
    could reel & blunder down the hall.
The hideous fate awaiting me!
    I sobbed—weaved on, appalled.

In years to come fell demon rum
      steadied shattered nerves.
I fasted: became a brittle twig;
      reflected, as death neared

great-great grandpa would never dine
      upon the flesh he'd hoped
would sustain him in his fetid lair—
      I went up in flame & smoke.

On Reading Poe

Josh Maybrook

Each night that I encounter Poe anew,
Dæmonic visions flash upon my mind,
Glimpsed fleetingly as though descried behind
A veil that hides another world from view:
Remote unearthly shadows, raven-hued.

All night, I read aloud the words that flow
Like music from the lips of some strange god,
Like darkly fragrant wine from lands abroad;
And though, at length, the sun begins to glow,
Night lingers yet within the tales of POE.

Cats Which Walk in Dreams

Linn Donlon

Cats—cats—cats—cats!
Indoors they disarrange my mats.
Outdoors they bring me wounded rats.
The small ones sleep inside my hats.
Obstreperous—yet for all that
I should not live without a cat.

Miss Midnight is the one who seems
Most skilfully to walk in dreams.
How often have I seen her there,
Sprawled out across the Dreamer's Stair!

And then I find her in my chair,
A whiff of Ulthar in the air,
Retiring when we see the sun,
As if a nightly work were done.

The big orange tomcat Maximus,
So patient, never makes a fuss—
I saved him from a sudden end;
He thought a gug might be his friend.

And then there's little Jelly Roll,
A calico of tender soul.
She swore that she would be my guide;
When we met ghouls, she hid and cried.

Though none will tell me what they see
In dreams when they are not with me,
I do not mind; it will suffice,
Their gifts of purrs and bleeding mice.

How the World Ends

Melissa Ridley Elmes

T. S. Eliot said
This is the way the world ends
Not with a bang but a whimper.
But really, the world ends
with a group of friends sharing shots of whiskey,
toasting Armageddon,
dancing in the glow of human failure
tipsy and twirling into annihilation
—radioactive disco of doom—
while the moon shines on, reflecting the sun
against our faces as we dance and drink and cheer
unaware we're already in the past
that's coming to catch us, ready or not.

When Cyber Things Return

Maxwell I. Gold

Thrashing inside my skull were the awful noises of my life, puerile thoughts trapped in pods of glass and gold, where metal chambers now emptied of gaseous nightmares, laid bare the most sinister iniquities. Bodies drained of water, carcasses floating atop oceans thick with sand and blood like lifeless mineral worlds whirled around a dying star that was my brain; dancing wildly inside an unholy cranial temple, where fissures prepared to rip open the exposed organ to an unforgiving, crumbling existence. Ignorant to the meaning of time, I had long wandered these halls of useless flesh, languishing in the banality of putrid fantasy, hoping for the day when the stars might collapse leaving me weightless, empty, and gluttonously feted, like entropy's sweet little plaything.

There in the distance, scratching the decayed bottom of some nebulous sky, the fingers of a city lost in name, but all too familiar in sight and bone; where the sounds of Cyber Things exploded above silver forges once filled with liquescent dreams, and overflowed onto the wispy, grey boulevards of my imagination. Now, the barren Cyclopean waste stretched wide as if the lips from some dead beast kissing the plane whereupon I found myself asphyxiated by the last memories of world I'd never see again, sockets empty of vision and thought, placated and humbled before the Cyber Things.

Harder and harder it was to breathe, to think, gripped by the syrupy bile flooding the calcified alleyways, as cerebral structures tumbled into darkness as a sharp paresthesia gutted my body. Pallid flesh and light soon decomposed into dust and dread under the corpulence of night, while lullabies of sweet entropy carried me off towards oblivion; thrashing inside my cracked skull were the last awful noises of my life.

Zephyr's Allure

Scott J. Couturier

A lonely idyll beside the lake—
aspens droop in late August's daze as
cicadas trill for ailing Summer's sake,
sky shot with sun-ray's succulence.

I espy a quiver above the water—
shiver of ethereal forms in dance.
Maids of pollen-down, fey daughters
of Summer's subtly ebbing trance.

I watch as they trip over lily-pads,
vitalized by slow & solemn gusts
of fair season's ending, ever-sad:
leaves fleck the lake with flakes of rust.

I feel the reverie of a faerie-dream
overcome me as I observe their spell.
Perfumes from worlds beyond the seam
of waking life lure me to blissful dwell

in kingdoms wrought of airy space,
where cornices of scalloped cloud
array opaline palaces of an elder race,
courts where no human thing is allowed.

Except—when the invitation is given,
one may shed mortality's immodest guise
& from its ailments forever be riven,
a guest of Mab with dew-dazzled eyes.

My heart beats faster as they drift near,
fragrant breeze a kiss upon gaping lips.
Yet, I ken also the clammy kiss of fear
as I see grinning skulls girt at their hips.

Five maids in all, of susurrus & down,
whispering sweet tones of zephyr's allure.
I tremble as they raise up a woven crown
of reeds, reeking with rank air impure.

Only then does that fearsome drowse
of pixie-torpor strike from my limbs.
With a cry their coronation I disavow:
each skull wears a selfsame diadem!
Another woeful gust, & I am alone again.

The Squire of Sweven

Adam Bolivar

Like Orpheus, I strummed a lyre
    Beside a crumbling wall
In darkest night before a fire,
    And dreamt of Sweven Hall . . .

A manor house of bricks and stone
    Once stood upon this place,
Where Black Jack Sweven lived alone,
    A sneer upon his face.

The Scourge of Devon he was called,
    A blight upon the land;
His actions left the priest appalled
    And from the churchyard banned.

His library held ancient books
    Of alchemy and lore;
The townsfolk shot him furtive looks,
    Except the village whore,

Who called on him at Sweven Hall
    To practice fiendish rites;
Black magic did their flesh enthrall,
    Consuming seven nights.

The scarlet woman then he killed,
    The climax of his spell,
A wicked act of lust which thrilled,
    And damned his soul to Hell.

The Squire of Sweven soon was hanged
    Upon a gallows tree;
The moon which rose that night was fanged,
    While Satan howled with glee.

And now the children all do sing,
While dancing gaily in a ring:

    Squire Sweven,
    Scourge of Devon,
    Went to Hell
    And not to Heaven.

Whispers from a Crematory Skull

Manuel Pérez-Campos

Behind the façade of provincial
welcomes half-obliterated by poison
rain is a brain-putrefying hell rooted
in maggots: exuding ponderous
silence, that vagary of the dead,
the once self-assured characters ill-
engaged by the thwarted expositors
of these miasmal topographies prefer
not to speak: an arch-nightmare threads
through this extremophile heptad
of evil rhapsodies like a river far flung
of which each is darkling tributary
and temporary detour: and as you
penetrate further, a cumulative
underhanded beleaguering of ideatum
to supplement one's fragile construct
of reality turns each at its core
hydra-headed and imbrued with
many-dimensioned phantasmagoric

fluidity~until nightside intelligences
spawned from primitive particles and
mired in starwind flow opulently out
of a transfinite gulf opening between paused
fingertips to crumble hamlet strongholds,
those sojourns of wayward sublunary
illusion, whether landlocked or by seaside.

Author's Note: The reference is to one of my first encounters as a youth
with the work of H. P. Lovecraft—namely, the Lancer Books 1969
paperback *The Colour out of Space and Others,* which features a skull
enswathed in decadent flames as cover art.

Unrepaired

DJ Tyrer

"You have seized the throne
And the empire.
Woe! woe to you
Who are crowned
With the crown
Of the King in Yellow!"
And, at that point,
Your fate is sealed.
Wrestled away,
Incarcerated,
Deemed insane.
You are a king
Amongst men:
Amongst men
Who are raving lunatics
Your triumph
Is as bitter as ashes;
Unrecognised;
Unheeded.
You are but
A broken vessel;
Unrepaired;
Your reputation
Sullied
And soiled.
All is lost.

Note: The first six lines are the final sentences of "The Repairer of
Reputations" by Robert W. Chambers.

Of the Swordsman of Words and Worlds: Eldritchard

In Memory of Richard L. Tierney

Charles Lovecraft

The Mason man has lately left this world
Though surely to Kadath to fight Old Ones,
With road full strewn with conquests and old bones
That he has left behind through chaos hurled.
There was a time, when through thick stars he swirled
Upon the wings of timelessness, and thrones
Of Eld begemmed with cosmic jewels like suns,
Which he recouped with sword-hilts, finely curled.

And yet his voyagings have never ceased;
Unearthly strange beginnings was he from,
Whilst in the shining spheres his chaos drum
Beat all the dooms from Azathoth, Cthul's priest.
The sagas shall not pause for Taggart man
As his strange visor greets great Simon's plan!

Classic Reprints

Funeral of a Vampire

Lilith Lorraine

How sibilant the silence
Of the dead who cannot die,
How smug the hollow ritual
Beneath a leaden sky.

How grim the plumed procession—
Perhaps the horses see
They go upon a journey
Into futility.

For That the hearse must carry
Along the funeral track,
Too vile for Hell's receiving
Will soon be coming back.

How thin the mourner's voices,
How strange the requiem toll,
How heavy is the coffin
That's weighted down with soul.

[First published in Lorraine's *Wine of Wonder* (Book Craft, 1952).]

Vampire

Bertrande Harry Snell

Up from the moor came Guldah, with laughter in her eyes,
And oh! her skin was like the snow that on the Jungfrau lies,
And oh! her form was perfect as mortal form can be;
Up from the moor came Guldah, like Venus from the sea.

The mist hung dank and heavy above the reeking sod,
A dark and evil vapor, breath of a fallen god;
Each rotting hulk and carcass, that in the foul tarn lay,
Gave forth a slobbering, slithering sigh, as Guldah came that day.

Up from the moor came Guldah, the souls of men to kill,
And oh! she bent the strongest to answer to her will:
Her laughing eyes made promise—they promised, but they lied—
She took men to her bosom, she kissed them and they died!

For on the lips that Guldah kissed, the beast-mark could be seen,
Mark of the awful vampire that hid 'neath beauty's screen;
Up from the moor came Guldah, her lips a scarlet pout,
But oh! her teeth were were-teeth, to let men's life-blood out!

Back to the moor went Guldah when she had drunk her fill
Of the red, red milk she needed to keep her devil still;
And the yawning hell-pit opened and the ghastly vapors curled,
While fast and ever faster the bat-winged goblins whirled.

Up from the moor comes Guldah, whene'er her devil stirs;
And I who saw her beauty, am waiting to be hers,
And I, who know her laughter is but a vampire's lie,
Still wait for Guldah's vampire kiss—one kiss, and then I die!

[First published in *Weird Tales* 13, No. 6 (June 1929): 858. Thanks to Leigh Blackmore for providing the texts of both of these poems.]

Articles

R. H. Barlow and the Activist Poets: How Did They Meet?

Marcos Legaria

Yet ever my gaze returns
Upward, to the fallow fields
And the chill soil
Where is nourishment for no crop.
Like a bead of dew
Slid from the flower of a dancer thirsting for air,
That star reposes
On the balustrade.
On which star is your throne?
How shall I search them all?

[Barlow's first Activist poem, Fall 1939][1]

R. H. Barlow's association with the "Activist" poets has been written about at some length by Kenneth W. Faig, Jr.[2] and by Massimo Berruti.[3] The founders of the Activist poets, Lawrence Hart[4] and his wife Jeanne

1. R. H. Barlow, *Eyes of the God: The Weird Fiction and Poetry of R. H. Barlow*, ed. S. T. Joshi, Douglas A. Anderson, and David E. Schultz (New York: Hippocampus Press, 2002), 173–74.

2. Kenneth W. Faig, Jr., *The Unknown Lovecraft* (New York: Hippocampus Press, 2009), 209–16.

3. Massimo Berruti, *Dim-Remembered Stories: A Critical Study of R. H. Barlow* (New York: Hippocampus Press, 2010), 333–94.

4. Lawrence Hart, *Poetry* 78 (May 1951).

McGahey Hart,[5] and Rosalie Moore have also provided their memories of Barlow.[6] What has not been specifically called to attention is how, and when, Barlow came across the Activist poets. Faig at one time was researching a biography of Barlow in the early 1970s. Faig wrote to Barlow's fellow Activist poet and friend Rosalie Moore, in a letter dated 8 September 1971:

> I am most eager to have any random reminiscences of Bob which any members of the former Activist circle might be willing to set down for me. Of course, I realize that the interpretation of Bob as a poet must rest solidly upon his work; further, that old acquaintances cannot be expected to write long, carefully constructed memoirs for the benefit of a work yet in progress but there in fact remains an entire area of biographical detail in which even the most random factual recollections would be of the greatest aid to me. How did Bob first come to meet the Activist poets?[7]

Moore responded to Faig a month later, on 10 October:

> I believe contact between Bob Barlow and I came through Florence Keene, a San Franciscan who was much in contact with poets through a small poetry magazine (I believe) she founded called *WESTWARD*. At one point during the year that the World's Fair opened on Treasure Island (that would be I guess 1940 or 1941) she wrote me a note about Robert Barlow's coming to the San Francisco area: whether she knew of him as an artist and writer, or whether she was acquainted with a member of his family I can't say, but she suggested he would be an interesting person for me to meet. Dropping Barlow a note (or vice versa) and talking by phone, we arranged to meet on Treasure Island at a literary program to which I was going; after that he went with me to a class in poetry that Lawrence Hart was teaching . . . I believe Technical

---

5. McGahey, letter to H. Leon Abrams Jr. (9 August 1980); ms., private collection of John Hart.

6. Rosalie Moore, *Accent on Barlow: A Commemorative Anthology*, ed. Lawrence Hart (San Jose, CA: Privately printed, 1962).

7. Faig, letter to Rosalie Moore (8 September 1971); ms., John Hay Library (hereafter JHL).

High School in Oakland,[8] and his association with the Activist Poets was under way. As I always understood it, and although he had written other things before then, his poetry career really began at that time.[9]

Barlow's poetry up to this time was heavily influenced by the classical and formal style of his mentor, H. P. Lovecraft. Now, Barlow was looking forward to a modernistic and experimental approach. The figure that put Barlow on this path began with Florence R. Keene (1878–1950), a Californian poet who was the founder, publisher, and once editor of *Westward*, a magazine of verse (1927–34).[10] One more mystery remained: How did Barlow meet Florence Keene? The following letters can piece these bits together.

A first trip to Mexico in the summer of 1938 signaled the end of Barlow's art studies. Then in the fall of 1938, while staying with the Beck brothers in Lakeport, California, Barlow made a first visit to San Francisco in November.[11] By January 1939, he had moved to San Francisco, and in the summer he rented a home with Groo Beck where they published a book of poems by George Sterling, *After Sunset*, issued by bookseller John Howell. Faig provided another key to the solving of this puzzle when he wrote to Groo's brother Claire Beck, requesting the names of any writers Barlow may have contacted in the Bay Area. Claire

---

8. John Hart found the following citation in his father's Lawrence Hart's archive: "Oakland Public Schools permit to use room in School Building. It's dated 3-14-37." (Personal communication with author.) I would like to thank John Hart for sharing some of his father's archives dealing with Barlow and the Activists in general.

9. Moore, letter to Kenneth W. Faig Jr. (10 October 1971); ms., JHL.

10. The papers of Florence Keene are held at the Huntington Library (San Marino, CA). My appreciation goes out to librarian Natalie Russell for supplying letters by Barlow and Rosalie Moore to Florence Keene.

11. S. T. Joshi's edition of Barlow's *On Lovecraft and Life* (West Warwick, RI: Necronomicon Press, 1992) includes Barlow's unfinished autobiography, which has the following entry: "*Transition*. Y.M.C.A. Hotel, *San Francisco, Spring* 1939. Once when I was in Lakeport I took a week or two off and visited San Francisco, living in the YMCA Hotel on Turk Street" (22).

sent Faig a list of individuals on 23 March 1972.[12] One name that stood out was science fiction author, poet, and editor Stanton A. Coblentz (1896–1982).[13] Coblentz wrote to Florence Keene on 5 October 1939:

> Dear Florence:
>
> This will introduce Mr. Robert Barlow, who called upon me this afternoon stating that he was eager to become introduced to some of the poets in the San Francisco vicinity. It occurred to me that, since you know many more of the San Francisco poets than I do, you might be able to assist in this respect. In any case, I trust you will not mind my sending him in your direction.[14]

Barlow in his teenage years contacted many luminaries in the fantasy, science fiction, and weird fiction field, asking for their autographs and manuscripts. He contacted Florence Keene within a month of meeting Coblentz on 14 November 1939, while he was a student at the Polytechnic Institute in San Francisco:

> Dear Miss Keene;
>
> Thanks for the Sterling poem—which I'm pretty sure is his, even though untypical—because I'd swear to having seen it some place before. Goodness knows where. Do you want the copy back?
>
> I hope I can get over and see you from time to time. My studies keep me hopping nowadays, so I am perforce unsociable! The Writer's Club dinner Nov. 7 was highly enjoyable—I am applying for membership.
> Ever yours, R H Barlow[15]

Rosalie Moore's letter of 22 February 1940 to Florence Keene gives us some insight on her meeting Barlow: "By the way, Bob Barlow is a clever chap. I think he has a great deal on the ball though, of course, a great deal to learn too – especially about people. But I'm very glad indeed that

---

12. Beck, letter to Kenneth W. Faig Jr. (23 March 1972); ms., JHL.

13. Natalie Russell informed me that this was the only communication by Coblentz to Florence Keene. (Personal communication with author.)

14. Coblentz, letter to Florence Keene (5 October 1939); ms., Huntington Library (hereafter HL).

15. Barlow, letter to Florence Keene (14 November 1939); ms., HL.

you had him look me up."[16] Barlow's last letter of May 1940 to Florence Keene details his current and future plans:

Dear Miss Keene;

Although I am tremendously flattered by your request I must reluctantly refuse, since on the 24 I have a dinner engagement already once postponed, with a Pan-American group. You see, I am leaving for Mexico early in June and have tied up much of my remaining time in Spanish-speaking activities in order to oil up my own third-rate variety of that language. All I can do is thank you, wish you very well indeed, and curse the luck which immobilizes me! [. . .]

The California Writer's Club,[17] which I joined under Rosalie's auspices, has a fairly ambitious program outlined for presentation at the Island this year, the first meeting at Pacific House May 28. I hope that I shall see you there, and in the meantime—renewed maledictions at the lords of the calendar—remain

Ever yours,
R H Barlow[18]

After this, Barlow would travel to Mexico City in the summer of 1940, registering at the National University Summer School and studying Nahuatl, the ancient Indian language of the valley of Mexico. Barlow would then return in the fall of 1941, registering at the University of California at Berkeley. When time permitted, he would join the Activist poets until his permanent departure to Mexico in the summer of 1943. Barlow would never again visit San Francisco or his Activist poet friends, although Rosalie Moore along with her husband did get to visit Barlow when she vacationed in Mexico City in 1950, a year before his passing. Since Moore was the first Activist poet to meet Barlow, it only seems fitting for her to relay the sad news to Jeanne McGahey, Lawrence Hart, and others of the Activist circle:

---

16. Moore, letter to Florence Keene (22 February 1940); ms., HL.

17. John Hart revealed that "The California Writer's Club is unrelated to the Activists, though my father (Lawrence Hart) used to recall that a large group from some such organization came to his Oakland class." (Personal communication with author.)

18. Barlow, letter to Florence Keene (May 1940); ms., HL.

Dear Jeanne & Lawrence—

Just a line to tell you Barlow died in Mexico City Jan. 2nd—overdose of barbiturates, probably not accidental. Got 3 letters today telling us. One from a neighbor there who happened to be a nurse said, "I did not know he was discouraged or depressed. . . . However, I'm sure you are well aware of the cause of his depression." Which of course we aren't, except to hear many innuendoes and to know there was some sort of serious maladjustment.

When we were down he talked so much about Hart Crane, making a joke of it and saying the Guggenheim committee had investigated their prospects very carefully since then to make sure no more of their Fellows would commit suicide in Mexico.

At least—I'm so glad we found him again. And we really did.[19]

_____

19. Moore, letter to Jeanne McGahey and Lawrence Hart (13 January 1951); ms., private collection of John Hart.

Notes on Contributors

Manuel Arenas resides in Phoenix, Arizona, where he writes his Gothic fantasies and dark ditties sheltered behind heavy curtains, as he shuns the oppressive orb that glares down on him from the cloudless, dust filled desert sky. His work has appeared in various genre publications, most notably in the poetry journal *Spectral Realms*.

David Barker has been writing supernatural fiction and poetry since the mid-1980s. In collaboration with the late W. H. Pugmire, he wrote three books of Lovecraftian fiction: *The Revenant of Rebecca Pascal* (2014), *In the Gulfs of Dream and Other Lovecraftian Tales* (2015), and *Witches in Dreamland*, (2018), all three of which will be published in German-language editions. David's work has appeared in many magazines and anthologies including *Fungi*, *Cyäegha*, *Weird Fiction Review*, *The Audient Void*, *Nightmare's Realm*, *Forbidden Knowledge*, *Spectral Realms*, *The Art Mephitic*, and *A Walk in a Darker Wood*. David's collection of horror stories *Her Wan Embrace* will be published in 2022. He lives in Oregon with his wife, Judy.

Leigh Blackmore horror fiction has appeared in more than sixty magazines from *Avatar* to *Strange Detective Stories*. He has reviewed for journals including *Lovecraft Annual*, *Shoggoth*, *Skinned Alive*, and *Dead Reckonings*. His critical essays appear in volumes including Benjamin Szumskyj's *The Man Who Collected Psychos: Critical Essays on Robert Bloch*, Gary William Crawford's *Ramsey Campbell: Critical Essays on the Modern Master of Horror*, Danel Olson's *21st Century Gothic*, and elsewhere. New weird verse has appeared in *Penumbra* and other journals.

Adam Bolivar, a native of Boston now residing in Portland, Oregon, published his weird fiction and poetry in the pages of *Nameless*, the *Lovecraft eZine*, *Spectral Realms*, and Chaosium's *Steampunk Cthulhu* and *Atomic Age Cthulhu* anthologies. His latest collection, *The Lay of Old Hex*, was published in 2017 by Hippocampus Press. *Ballads for the Witching Hour* is forthcoming in 2022.

G. O. Clark's writing has been published in *Asimov's, Analog, Space & Time, Midnight under the Big Top, Daily SF, HWA Poetry Showcase VII, Speculatief (BE),* and many other publications over the last thirty-plus years. He is the author of fifteen poetry collections, the most recent being *Easy Travel to the Stars* (2020). His third fiction collection, *Aliens and Others,* came out in 2021. He won the Asimov's Readers Award for poetry in 2001 and a Bram Stoker Award finalist for best poetry collection. He is retired and lives in Davis, California, surrounded by books, soothed by music, and enjoying bike ride excursions around town.

Frank Coffman is a retired professor of college English and creative writing. He has published speculative poetry, fiction, and scholarly essays in a variety of magazines and anthologies. His poetic magnum opus, *The Coven's Hornbook and Other Poems* (January 2019), has been followed by his rendition into English verse of 327 quatrains in his collection *Khayyám's Rubáiyát* (May 2019). Both books were published by Bold Venture Press.

Scott J. Couturier is a Rhysling Award-nominated poet and prose writer of the weird, liminal, and darkly fantastic. His work has appeared in numerous venues, including *The Audient Void, Spectral Realms, The Dark Corner Zine, Space & Time,* and *Weirdbook.* Currently he works as a copy and content editor for Mission Point Press, living an obscure reverie in the wilds of northern Michigan with his partner/live-in editor & two cats. His collection of weird fiction *The Box* was released in June 2022 by Hybrid Sequence Media, and his collection of weird and autumnal verse, *I Awaken in October,* is due out in late 2022 from Jackanapes Press.

Margaret Curtis (Master of Creative Arts, Grad. Dip. Transpersonal Breathwork, Dip. LIS), witch, writer, artist, healer, and activist, lives in Wollongong, New South Wales, with her family and a black cat. Published in magazines and anthologies, in print and online, including *Midnight Echo* and *Spectral Realms,* she is the author of four collections of poetry, including *Voice of the Goddess and Other Poems* (1991).

Ashley Dioses is a writer of dark poetry and fiction from southern California. Her debut collection of dark traditional poetry, *Diary of a*

Sorceress, was published in 2017 by Hippocampus Press. Her second poetry collection of early works, *The Withering*, was published by Jackanapes Press in 2020.

Linn Donlon is a middle-aged research scientist from a flyover state whose coworkers have been hoodwinked into thinking she is fairly normal. Most of her publications are effective cures for insomnia. She is currently owned by two cats, one feral and one sessile, and spends her leisure time opening cans.

Melissa Ridley Elmes is a Virginia native currently living in Missouri in an apartment that delightfully approximates a hobbit hole. Her poetry and fiction have appeared in *Star*Line*, *Eye to the Telescope*, *In Parentheses*, *Gyroscope*, *Thimble*, *HeartWood*, and various other print and web venues, and her first collection of poems, *Arthurian Things*, was published by Dark Myth Publications in 2020.

Rebecca Fraser is a Melbourne-based author of genre-mashing fiction for children and adults. Her work has won, been shortlisted for, and honorably mentioned for numerous awards and prizes, including an Aurealis Award and three Australian Shadows Awards. Rebecca's publications include more than sixty short stories, poems, and articles in Australian and international anthologies, journals, and magazines. Her longer works include a middle-grade novel and a collection of short dark fiction. The first in her forthcoming fantasy trilogy *Jonty's Unicorn* will be released in 2023 (IFWG Publishing Australia).

Ian Futter began writing stories and poems in his childhood, but only lately has started to share them. One of his poems appears in *The Darke Phantastique* (Cycatrix Press, 2014), and he continues to produce dark fiction for admirers of the surreal.

Wade German is the author of *Dreams from a Black Nebula* (Hippocampus Press, 2014). His poetry has been nominated for the Pushcart, Rhysling, and Elgin Awards, and has received numerous honorable mentions in Ellen Datlow's *Best Horror of the Year* anthologies.

Thomas Goff is the 2021 winner of the Robinson Jeffers Tor House Prize for poetry, with his poem "'Blind Tom's' *Battle of Manassas.*" Tom is scheduled to deliver a paper on the more diabolical aspects of Shakespeare's Prince Hamlet at a September conference of the Shakespeare Oxford Fellowship in Ashland, Oregon. He will also be reading at an Earth Day event in Chico, California, as a contributor to the anthology *Fire and Rain: Ecopoetry of California.*

Maxwell I. Gold is an author of weird fiction and dark fantasy. His work has been published in *Spectral Realms, The Audient Void, Hinnom Magazine,* and elsewhere. His short story "A Credible Fear" will be published in the literary journal *The Offbeat* from Michigan State University's Department of Creative Writing and Rhetoric. He studied philosophy and political science at the University of Toledo and is an active member of the Horror Writers Association.

Jason Hardy is an artist, editor, and poet from knee deep in the heart of Louisiana's Cajun Country. He is a lifelong fan of "The Alphabet Boys": HPL, REH, ERB, and CAS. His poetry is either weirdly humorous or humorously weird. His poems have appeared in *Ellery Queen's Mystery Magazine* and the *Hyborian Gazette.* He has self-published several poetry collections, including *Always Eleven: Poems Inspired by* Stranger Things, My Mommy Hates Halloween, Living Longmire, Cats of Cairo, and *The Paranoid Pirate.*

Chad Hensley is a Bram Stoker Award–nominated author. His most recent book of poetry, *Embrace the Hideous Immaculate,* was published by Raw Dog Screaming Press. His most recent fiction appearance is in the *Weirdbook Annual: Zombies!* issue. His nonfiction has appeared in the magazines *Rue Morgue, Juxtapoz, Terrorizer, Spin, Hustler,* and most recently in *Weird Fiction Review* #11 featuring his in-depth article on Cadabra Records. Look for more his poetry in future issues of *Weirdbook* and online in the Science Fiction Poetry Association's website *Eye to the Telescope* #42: "The Sea."

Ron L. Johnson II has received honorable mention from *Photographer Forum Magazine* and has been published in *Best of College Photography Annual* and *St. Charles Suburban Journal.* Since digitalization has put film on the endangered list, he writes now with words instead of light. His writings are influenced by science: art, fantasy, and the macabre. If he talked to you, he wouldn't stop, and his grandma nicknamed him Ronnie Radio. However, now his poems and stories do the talking.

David C. Kopaska-Merkel, a retired paleontologist, won the 2006 Rhysling Award for best long poem (collaboration with Kendall Evans), and has edited *Dreams & Nightmares* magazine since 1986. He has edited *Star*Line* and several Rhysling anthologies, has served as SFPA president, and is an SFPA Grandmaster. His poems have been published in *Asimov's, Strange Horizons, Mythic Delirium,* and more than 200 other venues. *Some Disassembly Required,* his latest poetry collection, comes out this year from Diminuendo Press.

Marcos Legaria is a scholar of H. P. Lovecraft, R. H. Barlow, Clark Ashton Smith, and related writers. He is a member of the Esoteric Order of Dagon and a contributor to *William Hope Hodgson: Voices from the Borderland,* the first full-length study devoted to the life and work of Hodgson. His articles have appeared in the *Crypt of Cthulhu, Lovecraft Annual,* and *Spectral Realms.*

Lori R. Lopez is a quirky author, illustrator, poet, and songwriter who likes to wear hats. Her Gothic-toned and extensive poetry collection *Darkverse: The Shadow Hours* was nominated for the 2018 Elgin Award, while individual poems have been nominated for Rhysling Awards. Stories and verse appear in numerous publications. Other titles include *The Dark Mister Snark, Leery Lane, Odds & Ends, The room at the end of the hall, Cryptic Consequences,* and *An Ill Wind Blows.*

Native New Yorker **LindaAnn LoSchiavo,** a Pushcart Prize, Rhysling Award, and Dwarf Stars nominee, is a member of SFPA and The Dramatists Guild. Elgin Award winner *A Route Obscure and Lonely* and *Concupiscent Consumption* are her latest poetry titles. Her collection *Women Who Were Warned* was published in 2022 by Cerasus Poetry; a full-length collection is forthcoming from Beacon Books. Her Texas Guinan documentary won best feature documentary at the New York Women's Film Fest (December 2021).

Charles Lovecraft is an Australian writer, editor, and publisher (as P'rea Press www.preapress.com). Charles specializes in the fields of fantasy and supernatural poetry, fiction, nonfiction, and Australian and international authors. His favorite authors and greatest influences are: H. P. Lovecraft, Shakespeare, Shelley, Keats, Clark Ashton Smith, George Sterling, and Richard L. Tierney. Charles has had more than 150 poems and essays of fantasy published, and has edited and published over 40 books.

Josh Maybrook is a writer, poet, and book collector from New Jersey. His work has appeared, or is forthcoming, in *Fiddler's Green*, *Grimoire Silvanus*, *Faunus: The Journal of the Friends of Arthur Machen*, and elsewhere. When he is not writing, he can be found browsing second-hand bookshops or exploring the countryside with his wife, Hannah.

Kurt Newton's poetry has appeared in numerous magazines and anthologies. He is the author of eight collections of poetry. His ninth collection, *Songs of the Underland and Other Macabre Machinations*, was recently published by Ravens Quoth Press.

Ngo Binh Anh Khoa is a teacher of English in Ho Chi Minh City, Vietnam. In his free time, he enjoys daydreaming, reading, and occasionally writing poetry for personal entertainment. His speculative poems have appeared in NewMyths.com, *Heroic Fantasy Quarterly*, *The Audient Void*, and other venues.

Manuel Pérez-Campos's poetry has appeared previously in *Spectral Realms* and *Weird Fiction Review*. A collection of his poetry in the key of the weird is in progress; so is a collection of ground-breaking essays on H. P. Lovecraft. He lives in Bayamón, Puerto Rico.

Carl E. Reed is employed as the showroom manager for a window, siding, and door company just outside Chicago. Former jobs include U.S. marine, long-haul trucker, improvisational actor, cab driver, security guard, bus driver, door-to-door encyclopedia salesman, construction worker, and art show MC. His poetry has been published in the *Iconoclast* and *Spectral Realms*; short stories in *Black Gate* and *newWitch* magazines.

Geoffrey Reiter is Associate Professor and Coordinator of Literature at Lancaster Bible College. He is also an Associate Editor at the website *Christ and Pop Culture,* where he frequently writes about weird horror and dark fantasy. As a scholar of weird fiction, Reiter has published academic articles on such authors as Arthur Machen, Bram Stoker, Clark Ashton Smith, and William Peter Blatty. His poetry has previously appeared in *Spectral Realms* and *Star*Line,* and his fiction has appeared in *Penumbra* and *The Mythic Circle.*

A career retrospective of **Darrell Schweitzer**'s short fiction was published by PS Publishing in two volumes in 2020. A veritable flood of Schweitzeriana is soon to follow from various publishers in the next year or so, including a new Lovecraftian anthology, *Shadows out of Time* (PS), *The Best of Weird Tales: The 1920s* (Centipede Press), *The Best of Weird Tales 1924* (with John Betancourt, Wildside Press), a weird poetry collection, *Dancing Before Azathoth* (P'rea Press), a new story collection, *The Children of Chorazin* (Hippocampus), and two further volumes of author interviews (Wildside). He was co-editor of *Weird Tales* between 1988 and 2007.

David Schembri is an author and genre poet from Australia. He is the author of *Unearthly Fables* (in collaboration with The Writing Show, 2013) and the Australian Shadows Awards–nominated collection *Beneath the Ferny Tree* (Close-Up Books, 2018). His poetry has appeared in several issues of *Spectral Realms* as well as in the *Anno Klarkash-Ton* anthology by Rainfall Books and issue 13 of *Midnight Echo Magazine.*

John Shirley is the author of numerous novels, including *Demons, Wetbones, Cellars, City Come A-Walkin', Bioshock: Rapture, Stormland,* and the *Eclipse* trilogy. His story collection *Black Butterflies* won the Bram Stoker Award. His new story collection is *The Feverish Stars.* His newest novel is the heroic fantasy *A Sorcerer of Atlantis* from Hippocampus Press. He is co-screenwriter of *The Crow* and has written teleplays and animation.

Claire Smith's work mainly explores other worlds: the mythological, fairy tale, the supernatural and more. Her poetry has appeared, most recently, in journals and anthologies including earlier issues of *Spectral*

Realms, Illumen, Eye to the Telescope, and *Riddled with Arrows.* She holds an M.A. in English from the Open University. She lives in Gloucestershire, UK, with her husband, the writer Oliver Smith, and their very spoiled Tonkinese cat.

Oliver Smith is an artist and writer from Cheltenham, Gloucestershire, UK. His poetry has appeared in *Dreams & Nightmares, Eye to the Telescope, Illumen, Mirror Dance, Rivet, Spectral Realms, Star*Line,* and *Weirdbook.* His collection of stories, *Stars Beneath the Ships,* was published by Ex Occidente Press in 2017, and many of his previously anthologized stories and poems are collected in *Basilisk Soup and Other Fantasies.* Oliver is studying for a Ph.D. in Creative Writing.

Jay Sturner is a writer, poet, and naturalist from the Chicago suburbs. He is the author of several books of poetry and a collection of short stories. His writing has appeared in such publications as the *Magazine of Fantasy & Science Fiction, Not One of Us, Space & Time, Star*Line,* and previous issues of *Spectral Realms.* In addition to being a writer, Sturner is also a professional bird walk leader.

Richard L. Tierney was one of the leading weird poets of his generation. His *Collected Poems* appeared from Arkham House in 1981. A volume of more recent verse, *Savage Menace and Other Poems of Horror,* appeared from P'rea Press in 2010; a revised and augmented edition is scheduled to appear this year.

DJ Tyrer is the person behind Atlantean Publishing and has been published in *The Rhysling Anthology,* issues of *Cyäegha, The Horrorzine, Scifaikuest, Sirens Call, Star*Line, Tigershark,* and *The Yellow Zine.* The e-chapbook *One Vision* is available from Tigershark Publishing. *SuperTrump* and *A Wuhan Whodunnit* are available for download from Atlantean Publishing.

Don Webb teaches horror writing for UCLA Extension and has been a top-rated instructor since 2004. He has been a member of Temple of Set for thirty-three years and written a great deal of esoterica such as *Energy Magick of the Vampyre.* In other words, he really does a cult following.

Andrew White is an aspiring writer who lives like a monk in the mountains of North Carolina. He is inspired by metal music, mythology, mysticism, and all things Gothic/Lovecraftian. Andrew loves nature, his family, and his books. He tries not to take himself too seriously.

Jordan Zuniga is an emerging Christian creative writer who actively writes and promotes on Instagram @cccreativewriter and on vocal.media as Jordan Zuniga. He enjoys writing high fantasy (sometimes a little dark for some Christian audiences) and speculative fiction. He has appearances with *Spectral Realms, Christiandevotions.us, Poetry Coloring Book: Halloween Edition,* and *Literary Yard* magazine.

www.ingramcontent.com/pod-product-compliance
Lightning Source LLC
Chambersburg PA
CBHW060804050426
42449CB00008B/1537